Slip

Cullen Bailey Burns

New Issues Poetry & Prose

A Green Rose Book

New Issues Poetry & Prose
The College of Arts and Sciences
Western Michigan University
Kalamazoo, Michigan 49008

First Edition, 2013.

ISBN: 978-1-936970-17-9 (paperbound)

Library of Congress Cataloging-in-Publication Data:
Burns, Cullen Bailey
Slip/Cullen Bailey Burns
Library of Congress Control Number: 2012940516

Editor: William Olsen
Managing Editor: Kimberly Kolbe
Layout Editor: Elizabyth A. Hiscox
Assistant Editor: Traci Brimhall
Editorial Intern: Allison Lee
Art Direction: Christopher Fox
Design: Luke Shrader
Production: Paul Sizer
                       The Design Center, Frostic School of Art
                       College of Fine Arts
                       Western Michigan University
Printing: McNaughton & Gunn, Inc.

Slip

Cullen Bailey Burns

10/11/13

For Isaac + Katie —
all best,

Cullen Bailey Burns

New Issues

WESTERN MICHIGAN UNIVERSITY

Also by Cullen Bailey Burns

Paper Boat

For my mother and father

```
  3176        3666
  2968        3647
 ─────       ─────
  6144        7313


  3420        3196
  3784        3816
 ─────       ─────
  7204        6012


              3724
  2532        4660
  3724       ─────
 ─────        8384
  6256
```

CPSIA information can be obtained
at www.ICGtesting.com
Printed in the USA
FFOW04n1037011013
1921FF

Contents

I

Involution

We will listen to the rain, the sun, the slight man
leaning against the wall. Everything says promise—
our teacups, our tulips, the silk tied in a woman's hair.
It's not so unbelievable, the calling out, the love. The box elder

has unraveled the beginnings of spring,
all these leaves, star clusters, shining.
Or we'll listen to the snow, the sounds it doesn't make except

in our hearts. And when the father's very sick
the child stands beneath the hot air blower at the grocery store
just inside the door, stands there in the noisy warmth.
We will listen, always, to time passing under our feet,

what the dead would say takes up so much space. What we
would tell our dead, what we do tell them, over and over
as the seasons change and we're promised to the future,

our bit of it. Beneath the blower a woman's hair ribbon flutters.
And the man outside against the wall, smoking and watching
the ladies pass, has a compliment for almost every one
in this light where every single thing is beautiful beyond compare.

After the War

Birds hold the moon up.
Had I known this sooner, perhaps
my arrows would still rest

in their quiver and the marriage
wouldn't have tumbled so,
bloodied, trailing a little light.

We Just Want It to Be Healthy

Here is the little bomb. We call it baby,
all mouth and potential. We do not speak
of disappointments—no one to strap it on yet
and cross the border, the demilitarized zone
of our foyer.

The neighbors coo at it, rub the tops
of its dimpled hands with their thumbs
and say, "give me a smile."
We think about schools and such,
of course,

but at night when we lay our plans
it always kicks its feet from the bassinette
in the corner of our room, central to some
final detonation, central to everything.

Kneel

The doctor. The botanist. The piano tuner.
What I have needed in the 4 a.m. city light.
Oh plumber, come quick! And God, too,

though the drawn-out sound want makes
leaving the lips or even the eyes
precludes heroics.

Kneel while I take everything.

Except that cap, jaunty and remorseless,
and worth something someday, too, if it should come to that.

American Music

The lonesome dock the lonesome paddle boat the lonesome oak tree and then the other lonesome oak tree but not the swans. They swim in a long line and stare blankly when I call out *are you lonesome*? They hope for bread and watch my hands intently. Fish circle the dock and want something of me, too. A wide ring of perch and sunfish look up through the bright water. When I make a gesture with my empty hands they scatter and do not return. The sunlight is not lonesome for it falls on everything and we turn our faces into it. Oh no, I would not be lonesome if I could touch everything. But then, besides the lake and marsh grass and woman reading on the hill, there would be other less desirable things to fall upon: the raccoon carcass on the road, Jackson State Penitentiary. Those men call collect to women with soft voices who nod across phone lines. The swans swim away. I have nothing for them but questions and soon winter will be here.

Thin Poem

The narrowing of the spine: stenosis.
The narrow point of the arrow: tip.

Reduction in intake, increase in output:
the narrowing of those hips.

The narrow strip of land: isthmus.
The narrow space between us: kiss.

Redolent, leaned into, such ruination:
the narrowing of our aims to this.

The Empire of Snow

Pink, nearly, sky
Against snow's blue.
In this cold province

Ice holds sway
And girls in silver haloes

Skip downstairs
With nothing
In their hands.

In the west, more snow.
In the east, the architecture

Of rain, place where tall girls—
Nightgowns hung on hooks above
Their too-small beds—will go.

Having Promised Not to Leave

Say lit candle say long night say the way it was
or say right here, the swallow, the bruise, the
breast-thigh-back debate. Say no or yes,
say I will never change, looking straight
into my eyes, meaning it, meaning it,
even if it's what I told you to say. Say
cricket say rain say right there, yes,
say never say can't you see I'm on
a losing streak say stay say where
are you going where have you been
say shut up, yes, shut up.

Tense

Am smitten, I said, and the grass lay still,
and him on it, and I barely lied.

I couldn't stand his shoulders, how
they rounded, how the past tense

would have ached in them. The true word
never left its place beneath my tongue

as the sun cast down gold, September,
and the crickets sang,

telling us how the cold would come
from the warm tangle of our arms

and legs entwined in what?
We couldn't stop imagining.

I lay beside him, my hands cold,
wishing largesse from fall,

from the future, until our silence
opened the day wide (as lightning

does the sky sometimes) and he said
am? was? what does it matter with this thirst?

Silence

The dearth a little word contains—
skin, silk

purple so rich we almost
call it black on the garment,

the rustling, for-ceremony dress.
Like bride.

Magenta and fronds and groom,
the petals strewn upon the aisle

fade. But here at the edge
of a kiss the future pours

like water down their backs.
If we say nothing

I think
death has a smaller chance.

From August

thistle better than nettle
anyhow

down at tamarack
down at mosquito

phoebe, eagle

far winter
farther spring

thanks be

May Execution

So we've put the murderer to death.
The dog chews an itch.
Something is righter than before.
The people are vindicated.
The dog smells doggy.
Clouds move from the west.
When Pol Pot finally died, a man I know said
"the devil will take care of the rest"
and he meant it, his children long dead
in Cambodia.
Thunder in the clouds and airplanes too.
Leave it to the devil?
Better than the hand of man?
The dog licks.
The rain begins.

Combustion

When the house burns:
do you get the dog out? or did you say documents?
So much worth saving—stop, drop, roll—

will you remember? is there a plan?
Nothing's on fire, nothing's on fire, not yet.
But one wants to prepare with the storm coming

or the pyromaniac niece, the possible
electrical malfunction. Admit it, we dream
of time in layers, each with its own catastrophe,

just as we wait for the future to open
its doors on the brightest prize, backlit
by the beautiful blaze. Grab the dog,

grab the deed, the house is on fire.

Slip

I've already told of deer lost in the lake
and girls with their soft-skinned necks arching away
and even how *is* seems a trick some nights.

So to stand midway in this decade
midway (good Lord willing/creek don't rise, or worse)
through a life and to think there are words

for this! This is what I wore
in my dream last night: no pants. Again.
I just don't know what it means.

And there go those girls again, rushing
forward in high heels,
long hair teased high as the future

from their vantage point.
Look, my hands are out like white flags
I concede, I concede but daughters

are long gone into the spring air.
And here's that whole long strand
of *remember this* I keep wrapping around my neck,

which is pulling me toward earth,
making me into a dowager:
who would have guessed forgotten

weighs more than remembered.
But maybe not. I'm young enough, right?
And there's still a little wine left in my cup.

Your Business?

Montana's burning swell
all the way in St. Paul

and the tinder of the far
imagined firs

recomposes in air.
Pretty flare (could it be seen)

and recompense for beauty
is scorch. Ask Smokey

or the small arsonist with his
lighter and papers in the neighbor's

garage. Accelerant! High winds!
The answer: things that burn.

Maple Trees and Unexpected Snow

Winter comes, sometimes,
when we're not done with fall—

all this snow on the crimson leaves,
the mother sitting down in her chair

to die. This is not winter
proper but serves the purpose

of forbearance. And when we are empty,
the anchors of our bones

weigh us to the snow, the trees,
the silver light

obliterating the familiar horizon.

Letter after the Revolution

There was that fox, do you remember, rambling across the field because we were nothing to it and it didn't fear us. Then the moon and the rain and the moon and the rain. I've written all this before. Or meant to. Or told the parts the censors left after their thick black pens. The women here line up each morning with something like hope on their faces but we must say no. And who am I but a little bit fat official? You would say differently who love me in spite. Do you have enough wood? Are you keeping warm? I don't know when the world will resume the shape it held up to us to believe in. Soon I fear we won't remember what we want—some butter, hot water, a little wine. Somewhere there is a story, in the long days, in these words, but only the old can understand it, even as I write from middle age I can't see the denouement though I hope we will be warm then, and happy. Ah, but I started to tell you, I found wild strawberries last night on my evening stroll and a certain afternoon returned to me as I bit that sweetness. And somewhere an owl called out and you were wings then beating in me and we were young and everything was that one afternoon of sun on the skin and sweet fruit in the mouth, everything surged in, even from this cold place, even when I think I may have forgotten your voice.

Late Summer Garden

So much to want from fingertip
to next, desire's

two syllables in the meandering
path. Glossolalia,

tongue turning words in madness?
Faith? Love,

I wish I knew. You
in the foxglove, you in dianthus,

you fête of each morning,
what I rise for,

cusp of moon, grasped,
you babbler,

the raspberries have ripened to tell us
winter hovers:

are we strong enough to set
her icy bones?

Winter I

I have tithed to the church of nil,
pressed my bare hands into the snow.

I have asked desire to forsake me,
on my knees, alone before the window,
and received in return a view—

the irreducible pasture, the far trees,
the glorious world.

Winter II

In the languorous hours
when sun falls down for nothing but light
I have longed for touch without heat
the lambent fire of needlessness.

Song

If sun be rain
and spring fall
and the emperor wrench radios
from dashboards
then yes—his hands

be thus and such
upon me. If winter come
without chill
and his child rise
from this water

and satellites
just once be stars
then yes—I'm his.

As Men are Wont To

I never believed the sheep.

Neither did I believe him,
the story he told as I
cleaned his wounds
behind the barn,

the $500 he pressed upon me.

Fall Chores

I open my mouth the chickadee
and a whole fall day flies in.

Ah, I'm listless in the unessential Midwest, watching
a sparrow weighing risks,
a man moving his belongings
out of a house.

Why not believe in
the long marriage?
I will.

Or, sweeping the front walk clear of leaves,
I won't,
envy in my mouth too, with the hackberries

and school boys.

Nostalgia

Of course we are beautiful in our remembering—
how my hair fell across your chest, how the sky
was tinged with pink. Sometimes I believe
we rose out of our bodies then, but I am wrong.

These are my loved mountains giving in to streams,
to rivers, to the inevitable ocean. I cling
to the pictures I carry of them—the land's
slope and give, the way pines also cling

to curve and inclination and somehow I am back
at desire. I cannot say enough just what
the night air gave us, how the fog caught
in the valleys, at the lips. But the fierce shape

of memory changes each time we play
the movies our skin made on the bright screen
behind our eyes. Better these mountains now,
fields with deerflies and crickets.

An Explanation

Desire, hear the song, resides
by design, dear Hera, resides.

Keep the watchman's hundred eyes
open; swan, herdsman: see

the infinite disguises one god finds
and the world full of beautiful

women. Ageless, you cannot know
how briefly one body lives in another.

Desire resides until the song stops,
leaves us split, stunned.

II

First Summer

How strange, the by his leave,
the distances of his touch,
the unfrail faith with which departure
preached going and, corollary, return.

See my land? One white sheet strung
against sun, purple iris blooming
for forty some years. The world does
and does not change. His heaven must

be mountainous. My yard lies flat
and green beneath the sky. One crow
watches from the wire, rubs its beak
against it, meaning being my burden

to make. Or not make. He is gone.
It would be wrong to say I am alone.

Pilgrim

I shake his ashes from my hand.
The new world waits.

Oily they are, and coarse. One more state
in which to lie, to go forth from.

I have clutched at the transformation, licked
it from my fingers, the closest

I venture to belief. The modern mind can't help
its modern doubt. But here

he falls to pine needles beneath
the world of thought. Fair shore,

fair moon for setting out, fair moment.

Want

When X and I made love and the sky
unraveled its far off and persistent thunder
and our hearts asked ever more
of our poor and magic flesh,
we gave away the days like these—
imperfect rain through a canopy of leaves,
yellow butterflies low over the pond.
I for one am regretless. And he?
Would I find him if I tried,
if some night I woke with all that need
beneath the thin fabric of my skin?
Fitful rain and warblers, an afternoon
spread wide before me. Let's say
I am without regret, X.

Taking Care of Business

My brother tossed a scrap-filled dinner plate
through the kitchen doorway. The audience yelled
"more" and "again" and then

applauded. Corn flew and small ceramic slivers.
The dog licked the floor clean. Once my brother said
he felt he didn't really live at home

though every night he laid his fine head
on the pillow. He was a sad and happy boy,
and when the plate flew

sparrows turned up outside
the kitchen window to keep him inside
with their softly beating wings.

Papal Vision Screening

Dilating the pope's pupils,
affixing the corridor's light,
he will see the way to God's pure voice,
we hope. The pope's heart weakens
and breath and a million prayers
pass through the empty cavern of his mouth
as he naps in his impressive chair.
Then the chalice, the ophthalmologist eyeing
the cataracts blue and milky like the world.

*

My mother lights candles for world peace
while the tippler, my father, lifts his cup.
My brother packs his suitcase singing *sushi sushi sushi*
and my sister, remember, is dead.
Here in Minnesota I shovel snow
and tape plastic over my windows.

*

But you know, the pope loves us anyway,
in spite of our land mines and effigies,
in spite of our tendency to bear wounds
badly, to trespass, to covet, to lie at night
next to the wrong loved one,
loves us and before he dies
means to touch the beads
of our backbones to his lips.

Derision

I know a man who held a baby
against himself as protection from the world
which was us and we were bad.
Small, blond and smiling, she served
well to protect, though sometimes
we leaned in for a kiss. Where was his wife,

upstairs making a shield of the moon?
True we had drunk too much. Said
some things regrettable, lay down by the sea
singing *Davy, Davy Crockett, king of the wild frontier.*
He never set the child down, slept

the four nights wrapped around her,
the wife in another room. We understood,
shooting baskets in the dark, our complicity,
and even practiced, as he had,
smashing bottles against the wall,
glass falling like sharp laughter.

Cleaning the Streets

1

The street cleaner's brushes revolve three directions, east and west
    and north.
And in the center where they meet debris rises up
and disappears. The street, wet and brushed,
is clean, but every tree in this town
has a plastic bag stuck in its branches.

2

The sky is like honey today
and the clouds amble past, letting sunshine
do the heavy work of falling. And the man in the machine
with the brushes eyes the curb and road
but not the sky. The willow branches hang like
green hair. How small a memory can be—scent of soap,
the light cast from the hood of a passing car,
a sloping yard to pond where a boy drowned
so a grandfather took a backhoe to the dam.
Weeping willows.

Sixteen with Thunder

The violets tremble all day beneath
    the wind
        and a girl has pinned her hair up
from the nape of her neck.
    So hot and the storm's left
all this water in the air.
    The girl's mother says
        here are the nets of my arms
but the girl twists a strand of hair
    watches out the window for something
        to happen
and when the mother opens her mouth again
    thunder renders her words
        empty, just lips moving,
and the girl won't,
    doesn't want to
    read them,
wants to read instead
    the steps
        she'll take from here.

As One Might Say, Then

Suppose gravel. Or cinder. Some surface cut
in palm, in knee. Suppose when love goes
we could point to scars (how we rode!)
but nothing shows.

Winter hangs on the horizon. On my birthday
he tells me *you will never know*
what you want. Could we name the little rooms
of touch and so forth

gone glimmering now?
The bike wreck, the broken bottle: skin
stitched clean and edge to edge again,
marks from twenty years ago.

But of this? A mouth, a wound?
Or that's too easy—words
like gauze or iodine? I don't know,
except once I wanted him.

Uncertainty of Evening

Objects give. Or light, falling,
takes at least their edges—the yellow
leaves of maple trees become glow,
halo, above the field now circled
by a gray form, no longer
stone on stone for fence.

The birds' song falls from
dark trees. And, listening,
a woman on the front step,
dishes done in the bright kitchen,
retreats from the sharp-edged world.
The sky opens as light departs

the pond and the closed up
morning glories raise and shift
the little light within them. When
stars pull back the dark, she,
drawn again to the things of the world—
door frame, knob, screen

pushed out at the bottom, fraying—
rises to go inside.

You

I am driving
toward your arms, lane
to lane, the breeze through the window,

Highway 35 south to the four numbers
of your address, the unlocked
front door. Love, I've

broken bones and speed limits
and still come

south in the evening light
with the flower
I'll pin to your lapel.

Nightfall

The sun at the mouth of the sky lingered. As did we.
It was an evening for lingering.

Where was my sweater? Was your arm
draped around me? Where was the pretty girl we called ours?

Was it the wide bed on which we lingered?
Or at table, over wine? Was your hand in mine?

But the sky, that sky we remember. Didn't it encircle
the trees and streetlights,

the flickering bats and chimneys? The sky had something to tell
us, and did, must have,

but was it so long ago? Was yours the mouth
I gave into?

Because This Landscape Was Once Sea

In the pocket of a wave,
      the small sound of the aqueous world,
            reside the most loved loves—girl with a paring knife

man with a ladder. A sink full of apple peels
      in the middle of a continent, all these towns
         named for forgotten dead,

and what's memory anyway but an old
      picture and longing that starts
         back deep in the throat,

a man cleaning the gutters,
      a girl walking to school with an apple for breakfast,
         a map of the future in her hip swing,
            in the undulation, in air.

Not Even Grief

1

Trisomic, some chromosome the mother wants
to take back, commission, admission,
but here comes a ceiling spinning
(tornado 90 miles south) and the genetic matter,
the mitered edges of the flying-past
windowsill because the baby seems fine
because a town's blowing by—wind,
cradle, St. Peter falling in or bursting open—
let this child, please, and the sirens begin.

2

The world beneath the world is transitory too,
and the world beneath that. Some nights though
the princesses escape to dance, in white gowns,
in satin shoes, because they are alive though they are not
because their mother grows old alone and lifts
the cover of this one world to watch
through each translucent layer each plié,
each diaphanous turn the other side of which requires
the shut lid, the place to which the kisses led.

3

Or the world above the world with high ceilings
and all those forgotten rooms and the lost daughter
docking her boat on the Mississippi,
returned but silent as the toasts ring out
and the mother leaning against the window frame saying
I knew I'd see you again yes
while the skeptics in the other room shrug
and raise their glasses, gods in their mouths
just the same.

More Valuable

Flowers are thinner
than children

(such weak constitutions)
though children are brief,
too,

their skin fine as petals.

And when they die
mothers spend months in lonely rooms of
flesh/bone/breath/frost.

Mostly though they live
sturdy and unamazing

bodies of work.

Bust

Then we disappeared for a while:
        long acts require
long cigarettes, someone to keep track

of the time. Noir or not noir, love,
        the dog is ill again
and you've given up all the fun

you once kept beneath your tongue.
        How could I forget?
Don't you remember how night's

black stick snapped back at your
        footstep? How
we laughed then! How we found

enough ewes for the joke and
        surprised the gang
in their sleek cars and cologne.

But now, now what? I can't rouse
        your ire or catch
those bright teeth in the light,

can't feel you when we touch
        cause the sting's
over and the cops aren't circling

the house to trouble us. The era
        ends. But you must
stand up again, love, you must.

Fervor

Some kisses subtract known from unknown
until what the sky offers, what it seems to offer,

is lost. Each minute lived in longing
makes the next one slower.

Dusty-skinned pears, persimmons
ripen in the bowl. Some men know.

And falling to the drawn-out days of passion,
to arms, to the small

possibilities of teeth, I'd forsake
the proffered stars for ash, for this.

Mortar

1

We have hewn a church
from rock and a God too
to find in stone some silence
to contain us.

2

A voice goes out. A voice returns.

3

Because our skin

blazes we excavate the solid ground
to build foundation for the towering
faith will make of sky.

Black Hills

The kid should return. To the doctor. To the small box
she came in. Should give up the cigarettes and iron pills
for the arms of the mother who wouldn't let her go,

though somehow she slipped,
fast and silver, into the backseat of the getaway car,
driving straight toward the ruins of that great inland sea.

A Dream about Kate

Last night I said to her: I know you're dead. This time I won't be
     fooled.
Then we danced.

I had already fallen
down the terrible dream chute and understood
how fast a life falls past.

Cheers, she said.
I can't remember her voice,
how she looked or moved. We just danced.

Plenty of Nothing

Zero's the opposite of grief
(unless you count the word),
stands proxy in the place
of nothing.

Grief's palms encircle faces,
presence: what's gone.
A half-empty perfume bottle,
voice the answering machine clicks on:

"I can't come
to the phone right now...."
Zero marks what isn't there.
Grief is what remains.

Encounters between Emblematic Flowers

Anemone, chrysanthemum and heliopsis could be
these colors: soft pink, blood orange, magenta.
The field lies purple beneath them. We will call that sage.
We will imagine the wind, the dance, design
a motion akin to blossom riding the end
of a delicate stem. What do the flowers stand for?
Not Christ's blood, not resignation, but delight
in order.
                              There is a girl in the field.
She is very far away, so far that we must imagine her face.
Is she waving? She knows us. She has been lost a long time,
we can tell by her long hair moving
in the wind. She begins to walk toward us.
Feel our joy! She is returned,
girl we planted flowers above, primrose and lily,
pink and deep red, for loss, for taking care.
She sweeps the flowers with her palms
as she walks and walks and gets no closer
and though we strain
we cannot bring her face into focus—those eyes,
that chin, the certain arch in the eyebrows.
We think to call out to her
in her field of sage and blossom, think
of no words to draw her back to our
wide open arms.

Be This: Ma, again

then none—none—bone

break, disappointment

your voice, child, seagull,

lichen, too, and rail

I would mother ever

and again would

you were brought back to these

two and strong

arms in good time

Moment of First Cold

I could wear this silk,
could wear such mountain, such ocean,
such tall grass, wind-tossed, leaning toward water,
could wear the moment and say:
see how the snow falls at hip-curve,
at sacrum's slight arch?
see the water's push and pull along the back
of the calf? Or here, small cloud
riding the left shoulder blade, to say
this moment, this season, raiment all
the world is—the felt world, the seen world,
on the back, in the lung, words
falling onto paper, rustling like silk,
one similarity remains: the metaphor
to slip inside as the front door opens
and cold spills in.

Achievement Test

Finally, we say, laying our heads down on the cool wood table, finally the girl makes the grade. Look at the blue Minnesota sky ringing the bell loud. All the children pour out of school, little exclamation points. Bus #5, bus #11, mom in the blue car. Teacher says, "good job," teacher says "safe summer," teacher turns back to the brick building. We who parent children in this hopeful state sing praises of opportunity and quality, gather our children into our arms thinking, gift, gift, gift to me in the wide and glittering world. We sing this way after the weights are set back in the rack and the floor's swept, after the humidity's lifted from the dewy grass, after every possible measure of day's been taken, then we turn with anticipation and relief to the results.

Say

The unthrifty moon grazes
the tree tops, loses
some light there until
she's empty, the curve
of a woman's hip, and reckless.
Here on earth
the lilacs bend in rain,
drop their ruffled cones
lightly to the ground,
and a man desires that light
to rise above him,
his hands holding all
a woman doesn't say,
while caught in the elm's
high branches: the lavish glitter
of wax or wane.
Words. A way in.

Change

Once we watched a deer swim out into Lake Michigan.
Twilight and the deer kept swimming
toward the sinking sun.

Fall is in the air this morning, in the breath
that rises from the children waiting for the school bus
and its noisy rows of those

who were us, we know, looking down
into our coffee cups, and who will one day
be us again—early morning,

work clothes on, coffee steaming
from the cup. We called the DNR about the deer.
It was August. The sand grew cold

beneath our feet as the sun went down
and we stood watching. The DNR said it just happens
sometimes, the swimming out and then

the fear. Can't do a thing.
And here's the bus. My daughter is too old
to look back as she climbs up

in the golden light that makes us beautiful.
There's no one to call for help. The deer
swam straight at that sun.

Such transmutation: water, sky, gold.

Acknowledgments

Grateful acknowledgment is made to the following magazines in which some of these poems first appeared, sometimes in other versions.

Buffalo Carp: "Papal Vision Screening," "American Music," "Kneel"

Court Green: "After the War"

Denver Quarterly: "Late Summer Garden," "Your Business?"

Many Mountains Moving: "Nostalgia"

The Melic Review: "Involution"

Phantasmagoria: "Winter," "Fall Chores"

Poetry City, USA: "Pilgrim"

Rattle: "We Just Want It to be Healthy"

RHINO: "Letter after the Revolution"

Underground Voices: "Thin Poem"

Water~Stone Review: "Maple Trees and Unexpected Snow," "First Summer"

Zone 3: "Tense"

"An Explanation" appeared in *What Light* at MNartists.org

"The Empire of Snow" appeared on the website *Poets in their 30s*.

"Maple Trees and Unexpected Snow" appeared in the anthology *Beloved on the Earth: 150 Poems of Grief and Gratitude*. Holy Cow! Press, 2009.

"More Valuable" appeared in *Open to Interpretation: Intimate Landscape*, 2012.

Thanks to Beth Roberts for her brilliance in poetry and friendship.

Thanks also to my step-parents, whose support is deeply appreciated.

And to Emily, Maggie and Mike, my most loved loves: immeasurable gratitude.

photo by Dani Werner

Cullen Bailey Burns lives in Minneapolis and Sturgeon Lake,
Minnesota. Her first book, *Paper Boat*, was a finalist for a Minnesota
Book Award in poetry. Her poems have appeared in many journals,
including *The Denver Quarterly*, *Rattle*, *The Laurel Review* and
Court Green. She is the recipient of a Minnesota State Arts Board
Artist Fellowship, the Neil Postman Award for Metaphor from *Rattle*,
and has twice been nominated for a Pushcart Prize. She teaches English
at Century College and keeps bees on her farm in Northern Minnesota.

The Green Rose Prize

2012: Jaswinder Bolina
Phantom Camera

2011: Corey Marks
The Radio Tree

2010: Seth Abramson
Northerners

2009: Malinda Markham
Having Cut the Sparrow's Heart

2008: Patty Seyburn
Hilarity

2007: Jon Pineda
The Translator's Diary

2006: Noah Eli Gordon
A Fiddle Pulled from the Throat of a Sparrow

2005: Joan Houlihan
The Mending Worm

2004: Hugh Seidman
Somebody Stand Up and Sing

2003: Christine Hume   Gretchen Mattox
Alaskaphrenia   *Buddha Box*

2002: Christopher Bursk
Ovid at Fifteen

2001: Ruth Ellen Kocher
When the Moon Knows You're Wandering

2000: Martha Rhodes
Perfect Disappearance